MW01165435

Your Little Steps to Self Confidence for Life

Paul Bailey

http://www.ImpactCM.co.uk

Dedicated to my incredible Step Mother.
Bernadette Bailey, you are an inspiration.

FREE 30 DAY PERSONAL DEVELOPMENT COURSE

http://www.impactcm.co.uk/FreeCourse

Little Steps is an email course that gives you 30 actionable steps, one each and every day, to help you overcome the challenges you're experiencing in your life right now.

"Just wanted to say an enormous big thank you for this course. I have looked forward to the daily email, I've always appreciated them. I've learnt a fair bit about myself in the process and undoubtedly made progress in several areas."
– Simon

"It makes life more manageable so that you don't feel overwhelmed" **– Julie**

"An exciting challenge each day" **– Michalis**

"I'm really starting to notice a difference my little steps are making. Mostly in the procrastination area but also to some extent in confidence as I've spoken to strangers more in the last 2 weeks than I ever would normally. Thanks for making the difference happen – little steps is so easy to follow" – **Lynne**

http://www.impactcm.co.uk/FreeCourse

Contents

The Basics

Building a Personal Development Plan for Yourself

"The principle is competing against yourself. It's about self-improvement, about being better than you were the day before."
– Steve Young

If you want to accomplish your goals, you need to develop a plan carefully for yourself. This plan is similar to a business plan, except that it is aimed at your self-development, specifically for improving yourself personally and professionally. This plan will help you achieve your dreams and guide you every step of the way. Below are several ideas that may help you develop a personal development plan for yourself.

Complete a Self Assessment

Before creating your self-development plan, you need to assess yourself first. This will help you make the best plan based on your current needs. Make a list of your educational history, work history, strengths, weaknesses, goals, and abilities. It may help if you take personal assessment tests so that you can measure your abilities. Also, try to ask your family and friends to give you feedback about yourself, so that you can get an accurate measurement of your abilities.

Establish Strategies to Help You Learn

Part of having a development plan for you consists of learning something new. This is why when making your plan, you need to make sure that it includes strategies to help you learn new things or improve your performance, at least. This could be anything from being updated with the news, reading certain books, or even taking up courses on something that interests you.

Split Up Your Goals into Small Tasks

Having goals enables you to see the bigger picture of what you want to accomplish, and how achieving it will fit into your life. There are instances when you may fail at reaching your goals especially when they are too grand or challenging to accomplish. This is when milestones and deadlines will come in handy. So instead of creating a goal for a year, try to come up with a main goal and a couple of quarterly milestones that will support your main goals.

How to Make your Self Development Plan

Once you have completed your personal assessment and established your learning strategies and goals, then you can start making your plan. List your short-term goals and long-term goals. This could be anything from personal objectives or even career objectives. Make a list of steps that you would have to do to accomplish your goals and your deadline for when you want to achieve them. Once you have these things in place, then you can start making the necessary actions to complete your goals.

Monitor Your Progress

After creating your self development plan, the next step is to create a tracking system. A great way to do this is by keeping a journal. Try to update it every day and put a check mark beside each task you've accomplished. Remember, your personal development plan doesn't have to be concrete. It should be flexible and something that you can adjust depending on your needs. There are times when your goals may change, which is why you need to be open to revising your plan.

If you fail to plan, you plan to fail, and that applies to your self development, too.

Design Your Own Solution

I was chatting with the very lovely BrendaBoo recently on Twitter about coaching and why I never give clients advice. Brenda got it spot on with this tweet.

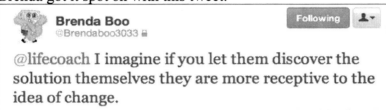

Brenda Boo
@Brendaboo3033

Following

@lifecoach I imagine if you let them discover the solution themselves they are more receptive to the idea of change.

I couldn't have said it better myself. I can't stress enough how much effort goes in to NOT telling you want I think is the answer to their situation. It all comes down to this:-

My solutions are based on my experience and my life, not yours, so it's unlikely that it will really be matched to your own situation.

Your solution is perfectly based on your own life and situation. Your own circumstances and abilities. Only you can design the perfect solution to your situation. I just help and support you until you find it.

So listen to the advice of others, read up and research your issue, but ultimately design the solution that is yours and yours alone.

Learn To Speak Positive

Often I work with clients that are incredibly talented at speaking negativity. When we first start working together it never ceases to amaze me how clients can put a negative spin on almost anything.

Teaching my clients to rephrase sentences in a positive way is often the first step to self improvement. Allowing yourself to work towards something positive rather than away from something negative.

One way to refocus your attention in a positive way is to consider first what you will gain from working towards and achieving your goal.

"I want to stop smoking" becomes "I'm going to be healthier and smoke free"
"I want to lose 10lbs" becomes "In ten weeks I'll be able to fit into my expensive jeans again"

This type of rephrasing takes time. Most people have been negatively phrasing things for years and it's not possible to just flick a switch. Becoming aware of it is the first step; learning to rephrase is the second. Finally you'll find it becomes automatic.

Practice makes perfect!

Compromise is Important in Every Aspect of Life

"IT'S NOT ALWAYS RAINBOWS AND BUTTERFLIES, IT'S COMPROMISE THAT MOVES US ALONG."

MAROON 5, SHE WILL BE LOVED

In order to build and maintain strong relationships, every member of a team or a family must know how to compromise. It is an invaluable skill that can demonstrate a person's genuine concern of the other person's needs. This act also shows his or her willingness to work together, whenever each party disagrees with a certain matter. Through this give and take process, all parties can feel satisfied with the results of their negotiation.

Learning how to compromise is important in a man's self development and maturity. A compromise is the middle ground of discussions, conflicts, and negotiation. In order to achieve this sense of balance at work or at home, you should learn to compromise with other people by finding a solution that could help all parties involved.

Why is Compromising Important?

There is a thin line between a healthy and an unhealthy relationship. That is the ability to have a give-and-take understanding between everyone involved. Relationships require much effort in order for it to grow and flow smoothly over the years. You can't just take everything you want, and leave the other person in despair. The same goes for arguments, you can't always win, regardless of how righteous your point of view is.

In the case of a business, employees and their employers should find a common ground in which to stand upon and remedy their differences. If each side acknowledges the desire of the other, they can come up with a solution that will suit them both. You need lots of patience and understanding, if you want to master this facet of self development.

What can Compromise Teach You?

By compromising, you can achieve self-development and be more aware of other people's feelings and needs. Sometimes people are biased with some of the decisions that they make. They base it on personal experiences and preferences, which leave others in a dire spot that can most likely start a conflict. By compromising, people can learn to empathize with the people they're dealing with.

When to Give Up?

The golden rule generally speaks about carefully giving to others. This goes the same with compromise, because some things are not just worth fighting over. In order for every relationship to work, you must be willing to make great sacrifices. This involves giving up pride, egotism, and arrogance at the same time.

When can Compromise become Unhealthy?

You must learn how to compromise for the sake of your own self development, but you shouldn't compromise yourself to the point of giving everything you have. Compromise, as you remember, is meeting *halfway*. You'll just encourage other people to walk over you if you give in to all their demands. If you become a push over, everyone will lose their respect for you.

Even if negotiations play a crucial role in a healthy relationship, one-sided compromises become unhealthy when they undermine a person's core beliefs and values. Remember, compromising is a form of balance. Without it, no relationship can ever work out at all. If you want to succeed in what you do, learn how to compromise with the people around you.

It's Your Choice To Be Happy

I was shopping at IKEA recently. It's not my most favorite store in the world but it was on the way home anyway and my husband decided he wanted to pick up a few bits and pieces. We were also hungry so we decided to grab some food whilst we were in there too.

Now I've heard that the company is actually quite good at looking after it's employee's. But what really stunned me is the young woman behind the food counter serving the hot food. She snapped at me asking what I wanted, large or small serving, fries or mash. Not once did she look at me. Not once did she smile. Not once did she make any kind of effort to interact with me any more than was the minimum amount required to get me to move on.

A number of thoughts flooded through my brain at this point. What would her day be like, if she actually tried being nice to people? Would she enjoy her work more? Would she find that people were friendlier to her?

It reminded me of a fellow podcaster Auntie Vera Charles. I chat with him frequently on twitter, well we normally tease each other actually, but that's another story altogether....

Anyway, Vera recently did a podcast where he talked about his face sagging as he gets older, so he decided to try smiling more. Just a little so that it would help tone up the muscles in his face. Great idea actually and something I would highly recommend! But what really took him by surprise was what happened to his emotional state and even the reaction of people around him. Others started to notice, even strangers commented on his happy demeanor. Just by making this tiny change in his face, he improved his inner wellbeing and this was visible to the people he met.

No one can put a gun to your head and force you to be happy, just as no one can really force you to be a misery guts. The choice to be happy is up to you.

What will you choose?

How To Guides

How to Find the Motivation to Finish What You Started

One day your life will flash before your eyes.
Make sure it's worth watching.

HEARTSQUOTES | TUMBLR

Procrastination is the number one enemy of success.

People set their schedule, write their to-do lists and set up their goals, only to procrastinate when the time to act comes. Even the best of us find it difficult to finish what we started. Whether it's because the task is difficult, time consuming, scary or tiring, people find many excuses to stand still and abandon their tasks-albeit for a few days (or months).

If your daily attitude is something like this, how can you develop yourself?

How can you succeed?

In many cases, a task that can be done in an hour is often completed in a day. A project that normally takes a week, can last for up to one month. Do you see the big difference? If you have finished the said work within the allotted time, then you could've used your extra time for other important things. The energy and motivation you had when you started the task was sapped by the forces of procrastination, and the desire to do something fun, or easy.

Here are tips to help you finish what you started:

Don't be tempted by thoughts and new ideas that pop into your head while you're working on a specific task. Instead, take time to jot a shorthand version of whatever you thought about then proceed to what you were originally doing. If you continuously flit from one task to another, you'll just feel confused and overwhelmed at the end of the day, and chances are, you didn't finish the important things you had to do. And even if you finished them, chances are you weren't able to give your 100% best work.

It's easy to say, "prioritize your goals", but what exactly does it mean? You might be saying, "How can I prioritize, if I have 6 projects due tomorrow, I have to exercise this week, and I have a dozen errands to run?" This comment takes us back to time management, and the question of what is most important to you. Some situations aren't as extreme as this, but it all goes down to one thing, differentiating what is urgent and what is important. Urgent tasks require your immediate attention, such as work deadlines. Important tasks have value to you, but don't necessarily require your time at the moment. Ask yourself these questions when you find it hard to prioritize what you should do first. If you have a long list of goals and tasks, mark those that are important and urgent, then remove the rest or schedule it for another time.

Remember what really makes you happy. People are often side tracked because of their urgent desires or needs. For instance, you might be working on spending more time with your children, and then you see one of your favorite movies on HBO. Do you sleep so you could play with your kids before you leave for work, or do stay up and watch it? Before deciding, ask yourself, "What will truly make me happy?" This solution also works well for people on a diet, for career related questions, and even for personal dilemmas.

It's time to stop wondering how the day went so fast without you accomplishing anything! Stop whiling and wandering about, get into action now.

How to Avoid Unnecessary Stress by Accepting and Understanding People

I'm sure you've noticed that people around you, even your family, are different from you. And when I say different, I mean different preferences, personality and way of understanding. A lack of acceptance and understanding can lead to unnecessary problems, tension and stress. Think about it, how many times you have asked yourself, "What in the world is he thinking?" or "Has he gone mad?"

To prevent yourself from stressing about unnecessary things, you must first accept this fact: Not everyone thinks or acts like you. Being different isn't bad. Things would be awful if everyone liked or did the same things, you know.

The good news is, you can fight stress and live in harmony with people around you. You just need to work it and try hard. Here's how:

1. Focus on today. Let go of past mistakes and misunderstandings. If you had a row with your office mate last week, forget it. Don't hold grudges because it's only causing you more stress and preventing you from giving your best at work. Aside from the usual side effects of holding grudges, it can also affect the way you interact with the person. If you had a disagreement with someone because of a certain topic, it doesn't mean that you're going to have a disagreement again with another topic.

2. Don't expect people to read your mind or know how you feel. If you feel ignored or if you feel bad, you shouldn't expect anybody to do something about it, or even acknowledge it. You should accept the fact that not everyone is sensitive of your feelings and thoughts. To avoid this, you should speak up if something is wrong and empathize with whoever made you feel bad. Asking questions will help you get to the bottom of the problem faster than skulking or silently cursing someone.

3. If you want to stop judging others, stop judging yourself first. We often judge or criticize people, even if we know that it's a bad habit. What we don't know is the fact that we criticize others because we criticize ourselves. Here's a good example: people often judge their co-workers for leaving on time or not doing extra work because they can't finish their tasks on time to leave early like the others do. Instead of putting pressure or stressing yourself because of your expectations, you should learn to accept yourself and your limitations. Only then, will you learn to accept those around you.

4. Stop labeling things in black and white. What looks right for you may not be right for others. Even universally accepted sins or wrong doings have gray areas for some

people. The term "white lies" wouldn't be invented if everything is strictly labeled right and wrong. Before judging someone's action as right or wrong, try to understand the reasons behind their actions. Use step 2 and empathize with them. Better yet, just don't meddle with what people are doing with their lives. Unnecessary meddling and judging causes unnecessary stress.

It's not that hard to live a peaceful and stress free life. All you have to do is follow these tips, and serenity will follow you! If you find it hard to accept people or stop criticizing them, I suggest you write down your thoughts in a journal. Sometimes, all you need to do is to let it out. If that doesn't seem enough, click the "contact me" link and let's talk about it.

How to Solve Your Problem in 30 Minutes or Less

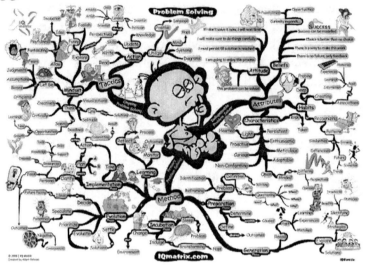

Everybody has a unique approach in solving a problem, regardless of its nature. Most people get anxious and stress over their problems for a long time, and this is even before they work up the courage to face it! Would you believe me then, if I tell you that you could find a solution for most problems in 30 minutes or less? This isn't a too-good-to-be-true solution; it actually works! Even difficult problems could be rid of using this solution in an hour or less!

Say Goodbye to Your Problems in Three Easy Steps

Step 1: The key to letting go of stress is writing. Many people would immediately shake their head and say no to this, but it's very true. Even people who didn't like keeping journals were relieved after they discovered the soothing effects of "ranting" on paper. Just grab a pen and paper and write all your thoughts down. No need to worry about grammar, or the words you use. The main purpose of this is to let all your feelings out, without necessarily having an argument with someone. After writing, you'll feel lightened and you will gain a fresh outlook in solving your problem.

Often, it's difficult to see the answers, even though they are right in front of you. This is because you get so caught up with what is happening to you that your emotions overshadow your insights. As you write, you will also detach yourself from the dilemma. Write about your problem, the details behind it and what or who it concerns. Don't think about possible solutions just yet.

Step 2: Write down all the solutions that you can think of no matter how impossible, time consuming or costly they may seem. In most cases, people already have an idea what to do to solve their problem; they just don't know how to go about executing it. This is why you have to write all the solutions down, along with plans on how you will execute them. Don't worry about how hard the solutions are, just write them down. Sometimes the right solution to deal with your problem may not be the simplest one. I'm sure it wouldn't be such a problem to you if the solution were simple enough.

Step 3: Put the paper out of your sight for five to ten minutes. Do not think about what you have written for that period. Then, go back to it and read everything you have written. This is where you get to become the observer, as you take in the words, solutions and the emotions that you have jotted down. As you read through the solutions you have provided for yourself, you will be able to choose the best solution for your problems, as if you were another person advising a dear friend.

After choosing the best solution, all you have to do is execute the solution. Don't worry about the solutions. The process may be long and arduous, but it will free you from your problems so just do things one step at a time.

How to have Confidence in Yourself When You're Trying Something New

It's typical for people to desire to learn new things. The feeling of desire and yearning for something better, something different, is practically ingrained in the human DNA. We all know that satisfaction is always hard to find. Yes people can be happy with what they have, but sooner or later, the desire to try something new is going to kick in. That wanting feeling triggers change, which is a good thing, however it often backfires when we're not kind enough to accept that we can't be good at something new easily.

Getting into a new environment can make people very anxious, thus, inciting feelings of doubt, fear and stress. Change is necessary, as is the difficulties that you have to face if you want to learn something new. A lot of people can help you learn and achieve what you want, but ultimately the biggest help will come from yourself. You should be kind and patient with yourself, just as how you will be patient with a child who's just learning how to read.

How can you Show Kindness to Yourself?

1. Trust in your ability to pull through. Confidence may be gained by how you think people perceive you. If people look up to you, you become confident to make decisions. But what if no one looks up to you? That's when your self esteem plays an important role. Self esteem is your own belief, not tainted by what others think that you can pull through and accomplish even the most difficult of tasks. If things look dreary, believe in yourself and remember the success you had with other seemingly difficult situations. If you're beginning to give up, remember how you eventually managed to accomplish things in your life, despite of the difficulties you experienced.

2. Avoid self negating thoughts. When people try to learn something new, they often think twice of their actions. Questions like, "Is this the right way to do it?" and "What if I fail?" often creep up. Doubting yourself will never do you any good because it destroys two things in you, your self esteem and your momentum. The euphoria of possibly achieving something is easily vanished by one negative thought. There are two things you can do to avoid this from happening:

1. Praise yourself consistently, even for little accomplishments. Praises and compliments reinforce good feelings into your brain. It's like your brain telling you that you're in the right track. If you do this consistently, you'll be able to build a new line of thoughts in your head- thoughts of you succeeding and doing well.

2. Make a plan and stick to it without questioning yourself in between. Asking yourself dubious questions while in the middle of learning something will throw off your concentration. Some even abandon their plans of learning something new, just because of one negative thought.

3. Accept failure graciously. No matter how hard you try to do things correctly, you will eventually commit a mistake. Remember that you're a beginner in whatever you're trying to learn, so mistakes are inevitable. Think of your mistakes instead as a path to better results. Some of the greatest minds in history won't be able to invent what we have today if they stopped at the first sign of failure.

You can learn something new and become a better, more considerate person by following those 3 tips. Aside from learning something new, these tips will also give you a better insight on your character. You'll learn about your fears, your confidence problems and doubts. Whatever you learn from this, will help you battle future problems.

How to Be Heard and Have Confidence Speaking in Meetings

One of my clients timidly came up to me after one of our meetings admitting that he had a hard time expressing his thoughts in group conversations and meetings. I understood where he was coming from because I have helped many people who lacked confidence with speaking in groups.

Just like him, I have clients who couldn't speak up, even if they wanted to be heard. Confidence is important in speaking, especially in important business affairs. Confidence, in most cases, determines a person's success. That's exactly why people should step out of their comfort zone and build their confidence little by little.

Tips for Developing Confidence while Speaking in Groups

Divert your nervousness into other things. Everyone gets nervous when it comes to speaking in public, even the best public speakers get nervous, too. The trick to avoiding any speaking mishaps is to turn them to divert your attention to other more important matters. Instead of thinking what could go wrong while you're presenting at a meeting, try to think of answers to possible questions people might ask you after the presentation. Doing so will prevent you from getting jittery, and it will also help you prepare what to say.

Practice, practice, practice, and practice some more. This is especially true if you will be speaking in front of a large crowd. You must know what you are going to say and how you're going to say it. Before attempting to speak in big events, it's best to practice with a few people, like your best set of friends. You're probably confident in speaking with these people, so all you have to do is practice what you're going to say to them, as if they were the actual audience for your speech or presentation. There is no need to memorize it word for word; the important thing is you have the gist of it so that you won't look unprepared.

Keep your words simple. Rather than trying to say too much, keep it short and concise. Avoid highfaluting words, because they're really not going to help you appear confident. It won't help you get your point across either. If you attempt to say too much, there's a big possibility you'll forget certain points, and the same goes with using difficult words. Worse of all, you might lose your audience. Make sure to communicate your idea quickly and keep it straight to the point. Jokes, commercials and sales ads are quick and to the point, and they're very effective at what they do. That's what you should aim for.

Focus on your audience and connect with them. Rather than focusing on yourself, work at focusing on your audience. Don't think about how you look like when you're talking or your body gesture, what you should do instead is capture your audience's attention and make eye contact with them. Don't just talk, and talk and talk, encourage audience participation by asking question, or even cracking a joke or tow.

Remember to breathe and act with confidence. The saying fake it 'til you make it is very true for speaking in groups. There are times when nerves get the better of some people. You can overcome this by breathing slowly and steadily, and then relaxing yourself. Even if you are nervous, people won't know that you are if you act confident.

By following these tips, you will be able to gain the confidence you need to be heard in meetings and group conversations. Being able to speak confidently is a key business skill that you must have, especially if you want to be doing business with the big boys. Use these pointers wisely to help you overcome your fear of speaking.

Questions

What Motivates You?

Why is it that some things you do, you have no problem in motivating yourself? Yet other things get continually put off.

In my website I have a coaching appraisal survey that allows people to find out the types of questions that a coach will ask and allows people to take some time and actually think about what is important to them.

A very high percentage of people state that they want to be more motivated. However, 80% of these people don't actually complete the survey!

Now of course this could be for a whole host of reasons, from being interrupted to thinking that the survey was asking silly or even awkward questions that the person wasn't really keen on answering.

I firmly believe that if a client isn't motivated then they aren't aiming for the right goals. Often I'll be working with a client one week and they are committed to completing an action over the next 7 days. When I speak to them a week later, they tell me that they have disappointed themselves as they haven't completed the task that they set.

Contrary to what people think, this is a GOOD THING! This shows us that the original goal that the client was focusing on has changed or isn't what they first thought it was. This type of inaction is a classic example of someone that hasn't yet clearly identified what is really important to them. This is why one coaching session isn't really enough to achieve your goals and make some serious improvements in your life. Over the course of several sessions you will find yourself changing direction a few times until you find out what really matters to you.

It's this learning process and re-defining of your goals that makes coaching so powerful. That is why I offer a Free Trial session. It really is a trial run and shouldn't be thought of as a one hit wonder. It all takes time.

Just like completing the survey on this website takes time. Even though there are only about 8 questions; they will make you think, so give yourself time to complete it.

Once you have completed the survey, why not book up a free trial session and experience a taste of what coaching could do for you.

Why does no one ever flirt with ME?

I used to date a guy who would constantly reveal to me moments when someone "cruised" him, or gave him a flirtatious look. I would drive me nuts. Not because I'm jealous, far from it. Much to my husband's dismay, I don't suffer jealousy anymore, I was cured of that debilitating disease many years ago, but that is another story!

What really annoyed me was to get cruised you have to be open to the visual signals that someone is interested. I'm the type of person that thought for ages that no one ever flirts with me when I'm walking down the street, or in my local supermarket. Until I dated this guy and I realized what he was doing. He was actively checking out other people to watch their gaze and provide them with just enough visual feedback to elevate a casual glance into a flirtatious glance, smile or even a sexy flick of their eyebrows. I realized that it was a three way process

Person A looks at Person B
Person B returns the look and allows their eyes to linger just that bit longer than a glance. If they really want to encourage a response then even the inkling of a smile should be enough. Person A either knowingly or subconsciously notices Person B is receptive to a flirt and if they are inclined will provide it.

As you can see from the above most of the work and manipulation is actually on the part of Person B. Now of course if Person A was particularly obnoxious then they need no encouragement at all. But hopefully you can see from the pattern of events that if you aren't getting cruised, flirted with or just generally a bit of attention that you'd like, maybe think a bit about providing the visual feedback, or body language that will encourage it!

Core Confidence

The Bad Stuff is Easier to Believe

"You look good today."

"I like your new haircut."

"We were really proud when we heard the news."

How many times have you heard variations on the above? You meet up with friends or family, and they pass comment on how you look, or recent events you've shared with them. Do you listen to the words, absorb them, and get a feeling of warmth from them? Or do you think to yourself, "Well, that's all very well, but what aren't you telling me?"

Why is it that the bad stuff tends to be easier to believe?

In our day to day lives, we come across both praise and criticism from a wide variety of sources. Family and friends, work colleagues, even the media. Whether it's a comment about our appearance, how we're doing at work, things we've achieved or projects that have fallen flat. Society has its own comments to make about body shape, how to dress, even the color of your hair can draw praise or criticism.

So why do we find it easier to listen to the bad stuff?

Compliments are good. Being told something positive about yourself, whether from someone you're close to, or a passing acquaintance, should really lift the spirits. Just the fact that someone has taken the time to let you know, should have you feeling noticed and appreciated. In truth though, how many of us really take these things at face value?

For many, being complimented is at best a source of embarrassment, or at worst, a thinly veiled attack. Have you ever found yourself wondering whether someone is simply saying something nice to detract from something terrible they don't want

to say to you? "Okay, maybe they think my hair looks good ....
but why do they keep looking at my coat like that?"

The world today is fast, furious, instant and demanding. The
pressures to perform well have grown, both in a personal and
professional capacity. All this brings an increased sense of
expectation that we have to be at our best, doing our best, all the
time. Which, let's face it, can be a pretty tall order.

So it's easy to believe that we can't possibly be doing well,
because of the pressures we are putting on ourselves. Whether it's
keeping up with the "Jones'" or knowing there's still that other
piece of work you haven't finished yet. It's like the day is never
quite long enough, we feel there is always something more we
should do.

All any of us can really do though is our best; to try and
acknowledge our limits, our strengths and weaknesses; to
improve what can be improved, and accept what cannot. And if
someone should say something nice, something good about us –
try taking it at face value and say "Thank you." And mean it!

(BTW just in case you were wondering the title of this blog
comes from a line in the film Pretty Woman) Vivian: People put
you down enough, you start to believe it.
Edward Lewis: I think you are a very bright, very special
woman.
Vivian: The bad stuff is easier to believe. You ever notice that?

Confidence and Goal Setting Lessons we can Learn from the Olympics

Goals are very important, especially for people who want make something out of their lives. Setting goals is the first step towards achievement. It gives you the motivation to become better in your job, in your family life and in your relationships. Goals give you the inspiration to take action to hit the ground running. Without goals, you will not achieve much in life.

Despite its importance, there are people who don't care much about goal setting. They're very impassive with their lives. These people don't think that it's important to set goals, which is why they just 'go with the flow' and let the circumstances run their lives. Then there are others, who set goals, but don't have the confidence to achieve whatever they want. These types of people start out as very eager, then lose confidence and start to drift off, eventually becoming almost apathetic. When that happens, they will just live their lives doing what they have always known to do.

Lessons from the Olympics

1. Even the most impossible feat can be achieved if you have confidence in yourself. Athletes get nervous too, but they know that getting nervous won't help them. Before the game, they condition their minds and put their game-face on. They replace whatever insecurities they have with confidence. You can do this, too. Before a big speech or presentation, take a moment to calm your nerves and reflect on your achievements. Doing this will increase your confidence.

2. Goals prepare Olympic athletes physically and mentally. Did you know that goals are used by sports psychologists in order to help athletes improve their performance? Setting goals and knowing what you want to achieve is half the battle. Knowing what you want to do gives you a purpose to work for. It gives you a good reason to strive harder. Athletes become more competitive when they know that they have a record to keep or a goal to accomplish. You can apply this technique to yourself by setting milestones or mini-goals that you want to accomplish by the end of the month. This mindset will also help you strive to perform better, just as athletes always go for the gold.

3. Proper discipline can take you places. Athletes wake up at the first light of dawn to exercise and practice their routines. Yes I'm pretty sure they would prefer to sleep in, but they don't. Why? Because they know how important it is to discipline themselves on training. Without discipline, they won't be able to run or swim as fast as they can. Without discipline, you won't be able to get a promotion, grow your business and manage your time.

The Olympics is one of the most popular and biggest events, and it has allowed athletes to set numerous records in the past. The athletes performing in their respective sports have dedicated so much of their lives into winning a gold medal, and that just shows how dedicated they are. Winners are glorified in their own countries, and their names will be recorded in history.

What about you? Do you have what it takes to win a gold medal in life? You won't find out unless you start doing something worthwhile for your life. Learn from these lessons and start now!

Don't let Criticisms Get the Best of You

Living in a world filled with people with different personalities, it is just natural to find others who judge you and say something about your behavior, condition, work, and just about anything they can think of. These criticisms can be great causes of stress.

thatonerule: #114

Be open to criticism but don't be affected by it. Criticism is meant to help you be a better person. Learn from it.

thatonerule.com

Criticism affects everybody at one time or another. However, the person criticizing you does not always mean you harm. Sometimes, people just say things to express their opinions and beliefs. Criticisms are not solely for pointing out your shortcomings and failures.

Characteristics of Criticisms

Criticism is directed towards a person, group, authority, or organization, as an objection to a specific kind of behavior. This is personal criticism that is delivered by one person to another, just like gossip.

Criticism is highly either detailed & specific or very abstract and general. One person can criticize your profession, while another could criticize the exact duties involved in your line of work.
Criticisms can be expressed verbally or non-verbally.
Criticism can be stated clearly or as sarcastic remarks.
It may be the product of critical thinking, but for most people, it is a spontaneous remark.

Criticisms of any kind are huge causes of stress, especially for the person it is directed to. There are 3 common ways you can react to criticism:

1. Completely agree with it
2. Resist it
3. Ignore it

Tips for handling criticism:
In business, criticisms are always expected when an idea or service is new in the market. Experienced businessmen and mature individuals do not see criticisms as causes of stress, because they already know that there is a link between anger, control and perfectionism. Use these tips to manage and handle criticisms well:

Accept the criticism and let it help you make yourself a better person. Listen to what critics are saying. For all you know, there is something good in what they say about you. Use their remarks as a frame of references.

Although it is difficult, do not be defensive about what you hear. Open your ears and be receptive of people's comments.

Avoid exposing yourself to criticism from people whose intentions are dubious. Their sole intention is to pull you down. Refrain from making an immediate response to a criticism. Counting one to ten is the wisest course of action. Your delayed reaction may save you from saying harsh things you may regret later.

Since most criticisms have a certain grain of truth, accept your mistake graciously. Don't deny it or put the blame on others. It will clear negative vibes around you, and help everyone focus on the things to be done.

Not all criticisms are the same; and not all are good or bad. Take criticisms as part of your learning process. If you feel that your critics are unfair; then roll up your sleeves and show them that you are the good guy. As long as you are in the right, you don't need to change yourself just to please others.

Do not allow criticisms to spoil your day. If you know how to handle criticisms, they will become your ally in becoming better and overcoming the causes of stress.

Productivity

Time Management: The Solution for not Having Enough Time

Time management is one of the things many people struggle with. It's difficult, and almost impossible, especially when so many different tasks need to be done. You need to work, do errands, make time for your family, and lots of other tasks, and before you know it, the day has ended without a single reprieve. Worse, you didn't even get to finish everything you wanted to accomplish for that day!

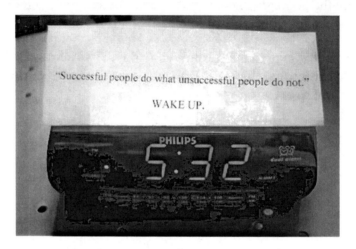

Most people, especially single parents, don't prioritize their personal time or "me time." It may not occur to you, but even a short break will be enough to soothe your mind and lessen your stress. Spend this short time reading a book, going for a jog, or doing something else you enjoy. But then, some of you would say, "I don't have time for that", or "I'm already too busy and I can't add anything more to my plate"

Personal time is important, if only to help you keep going in life. If you don't have time, the best way to create time is waking up earlier than normal. Sleep earlier, wake up earlier. It's not impossible.

The Benefits of Waking Up Earlier

You will be able to accomplish something for yourself – If you have time management problems and never have time to simply read a book or exercise, this can change if you disciple yourself to wake up earlier. Being up at 5 AM, before everyone else, and having an hour to yourself to do anything you want will make you happy. It will give you much need peace and quiet, too.

Time Management: The Solution for not Having Enough Time

Starting your day early gives you more time to accomplish things– Starting your day early and doing something you enjoy will not only make you a happy camper, it will also help you accomplish more things. For instance, finally having some time for you is a start. Aside from that, waking up earlier will give you a head start to do your other tasks while your mind is still working quickly! Time management can be challenging but once you find a routine that works for you, then you will be able to balance everything successfully.

You will end your day knowing that you had accomplished the day's primary tasks–If you plan to do something at the end of the day and discover that you just don't have any time left, you will most likely be left disappointed. If you start your day doing the most important things, then you will end your day happy because even if you are exhausted, you've already did that one most important thing for the day.

Tips for Waking up Early

Turn off the TV after dinner

Make sure there's absolutely no light in your bedroom. The lights from PDAs, laptops and alarm clocks can disturb your sleep.

Sleep and wake up at the same time every day. Even at weekends!

Don't read your emails at night, reading emails tend to cause stress, thus preventing you from sleeping on time.

Stick to your plan, even if you didn't get enough sleep last night. If you fall through, the cycle will just repeat itself and you'll never have the chance to wake up early for the week.

Waking up early is not easy, especially at first. However, if you continue to do it regularly, you will get used to it eventually. You will also have more energy to do things for yourself when you wake up early in the morning, in comparison to cramming to finish things at the end of the day.

You need to realize that it's not that there is not enough time in the day to do what you want; it is poor time management that is hindering you from doing things that you want. So what's the solution? Wake up early, it works! Try it for yourself!

Stop Over Thinking Your Goals. Start Moving!

"A dream becomes a goal when action is taken towards its achievement." Bo Bennett

You reach a point in your life when you wake up and start thinking about your life. You look back on the past years trying to find something to be truly proud of, something big you've achieved. Though you're able to recall a few, you definitely want to do more.

You stop and begin to review and asses where your life is heading to. You want a breakthrough—that big break whether in career or relationship that you've been dreaming of. You want to achieve more and do bigger things, something spectacular to give you that fulfillment you're looking for.

The problem is you often just stop at the thought of wanting to do it. You get stuck with just thinking about it—actually you're over thinking it. What you lack is goal setting and concrete action plans. Stop thinking about moving forward- do it!

Life coaching may help jumpstart you to slide forward step by step. Sometimes a little help from the outside can do wonders in guiding you through your goals. Life coaching will give you self help practical tips that will guide you with goal setting and working to reach them.

If you think about it, goal setting and achieving them isn't rocket science—it only takes determination and passion to step out and just do it.

Below are some very practical tips to help you move forward and achieve more success in life:

Make a pledge to keep your goal. Take that firm decision that no matter what happens you will pull through with your goal and action points.

Set your priorities before goal setting. Your goals must be in sync with your major priorities in life—whether they are your parents, children, a husband or wife.
Write down your every goal. It helps you remember when you write them down. This also helps you refer to them from time to time.

Don't stop with just goal setting, now set action plans. You're way past thinking about what you should do. It's time to act on it. Set action points towards your goal. These may take certain changes in life and even establishing new boundaries and standards. But it will all be worth it. So, just do it.

Be accountable to someone. Involving someone to help keep your progress in check may be very helpful.
Embrace failure. Don't give up at the first sign of failure; take this as a challenge to do even better. Failure is a part of the entire process of moving forward.

Celebrate your victories. Every time you achieve a certain goal and slide forward celebrate the moment! There are no small victories, everything is worth celebrating.

Don't lose sight of your goals and commitment. The road to success can be long and hard, but it will all be worth it in the end. So keep your focus on the goal that you have set.

Often times we know what we want to achieve in life but we just get stuck over thinking it and contemplating too much about it that we never really move forward. Nothing is ever going to happen unless we start moving. So, when you want to achieve something, just stand up and do it!

Find the Motivation You Need

Life isn't perfect. Often, it's not even anywhere near the vicinity of perfect. In this journey, bad times are inevitable—you climb over obstacles, bump into trials, are torn between crossroads, and stop at dead ends. But as they say 'Life must go on'.

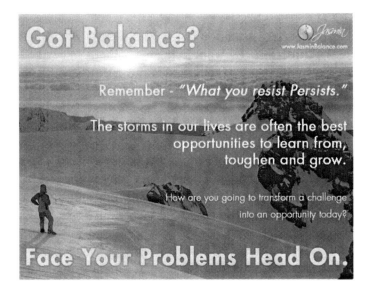

Quarter life crisis, mid-life crisis, and even economic crisis... you've heard it all! You reach a point in your life when you feel like you're not good enough. Deep down inside you know that you want more in life, but the question is how to reach it and where to begin.

Of course you want to change for the better, who doesn't? But you always get lost somewhere along the road. Then after a few days of feeling lost, distracted or overworked, you find yourself feeling down because of self defeating thoughts.

If you feel like you've been going around in circles in your personal life, then what you actually need is outside help to provide you the motivation and will-power you lack from within. This is where life coaching comes to play.

Life coaching will help you with practical, self help tips that will allow you to realize your true potentials. Coaching will enable you to recognize:

> your current situation in life
> the direction you want to take
> the right road that will lead you there

You need a great deal of motivation and focused action to begin your journey to a better you, and a more fulfilling life.

Below are some common life problems you may face, especially in your 30's, 40's, and 50's. Though they may seem like huge hurdles to jump over, really a few self help tips and the right kind of motivation will help you come out victorious.

You want to be heard. Now, who doesn't want to be heard? You feel stuck in a status quo. So it's the same boring routine for years on end. You want a breakthrough. You know it's about time to let go of your bad habits but can't find the motivation to do so. You want to get your priorities right. You face life's major crossroad such as a retirement or a career shift. And you wonder where you go from there. You've been seeking after that growth in business and relationship that never seems to happen.

Life coaching and self help techniques will allow you to find the inner courage, passion, and determination to set balance in life and move forward. You need realistic goals and guided decisions to achieve them.

But ultimately, change will begin within you. No one can change for you. Below are some self help motivation tips to usher in change in your life:

Stop and really asses you life. Write down realistic goals and commit to follow them. Stretch yourself daily to achieve each goal step by step.
Set your personal core values and stay true to them. Your character is better than your reputation—who you really are is more important than what people think you are.
Do your best everyday in all you do. Success doesn't happen overnight, but may be achieved through constant improvement.
Always see the best about other and be willing to help them.
You may have all the material success, but it's the relationships you've built and nurtured that makes life significant.
Never stop learning and be willing to build your skills.

All people can do to help you is offer self help tips and a guiding hand, but to actually act upon them and change is all up to you. Do your best and seek don't be afraid to seek help, and then talk to someone who can provide you guidance.

Top Tips

22 Top Tips To Building Confidence

A simple list of ideas to help build your confidence:-

1. Compliment other people.

2. Accept compliments gracefully.

3. Keep fit, you don't need the body of a god(ess) to feel good about yourself.

4. Keep a journal; it helps to calm a judgmental inner voice.

5. Recognize your insecurities; accepting them is the first step to conquering them.

6. Avoid perfectionism, good enough will do, tell yourself you can always come back to it later.

7. Take care of your appearance, and then it's one less thing to worry about.

8. Practice smiling before entering a room.

9. Learn a new skill to gently challenge you.

10. Listen to your doubts, but challenge their validity. 11. Reveal a little bit of the real you to people you meet.

11. Fear is a way of letting you know that you're about to stretch yourself and grow.

12. Scared of looking a fool? Remember to laugh with them, so they can't laugh at you.

13. Confidence sometimes means admitting you're wrong.

14. Sometimes the most confident thing to do is ask for help.

15. Don't compare yourself with others, they have a whole heap of issues you aren't aware of and certainly wouldn't want to swap with.

16. Being validated by someone else is not the answer to anything.

17. Being confident is a journey not a destination.

18. Seeing a task through to the end builds confidence, quitting because it was hard damages it.

19. Distract your inner fears by directing your focus on helping others.

20. Allow yourself to accept failing as a lessoned learned in the school of hard knocks. It's the best form of education.

21. Recognize your successes; don't be afraid to say you're good at something especially to yourself!

22. Remember that no one is perfect, in fact most are a lot less perfect than you

16 Tips On How To Be Happy

1. Be Optimistic: The world isn't against you, even though it feels like that sometimes. Recognize that what happened in your past doesn't mean the future has to be the same. Instead of thinking about why things are happening to you, focus on what you are going to do to get things back on track. No one expects you to be overly positive all the time, pretending that everything is perfect. So just accept when you are having a bad day, or you're in a crabby mood. It's happens.

2. Trust your instincts. In a study, two groups of people were asked to pick out a poster to take home. One group were asked to analyze their decision carefully, weighing the pros and cons, and the other group were told to go with their gut reaction. Two weeks later, the group that followed their instinct were happier with their posters than the group that analyzed their decisions.

3. Make enough money to meet your basic needs: food, shelter, and clothing. More importantly spend less than you earn. Material items only provide short-term happiness, where as experiences and the memory of them last a lifetime. Stay close to friends and family. By keeping a small close-knit circle of friends and family it's easier to keep in touch. Give time to the people who will be there when you need them most, rather than "fair weather friends".

4. Find happiness in the job you have. Many people expect the right job or the right career to dramatically change their level of happiness, but from personal experience, most of my clients that came to me with work issues ended up working them out and staying in their job, rather than moving on.

5. Smile. Whether you feel happy or not, your mood will be elevated. So smile all the time!

6. Laugh a lot. It's fairly well known that laughing releases natural endorphins. There are even classes you can take to exercise those laughter muscles!

7. Forgive. Holding a grudge takes up a lot of time and energy. In a study, it was found that an attitude of forgiveness also contributed to better cardiovascular health.

8. Make friends who share your interests, if you don't know any make a special effort to join a club or online forum. If none exist then create your own, chances are there are many people out there with the same interests as you.

9. Give lots of compliments. I use this one a lot in my coaching. The act of giving compliments teaches you a lot about how people react. What works well and what doesn't. More importantly also teaches you how to receive compliments.

10. Perform acts of kindness anonymously. Just the knowledge that you did something to make someone else's life just a little bit easier is bound to put a smile on your face.

11. Look after your health, stretch yourself physically and get plenty of sleep. A tired, sick and inactive body certainly isn't going to do anything for your confidence, self-esteem or happiness.

12. Don't "treat" feeling down. These treats are normally bad for you and the pleasure lasts only a few minutes. You may think that feeling better for a few minutes is good enough, but then you'll have to deal with the guilt later, adding to your woes.

13. Do something creative. There's nothing more satisfying than creating a drawing, doing some writing or creating something out of bits and pieces. Even if it's not very good, it's yours.

14. Keep a diary. Another one I use in my coaching all the time. This is a great way to externalize the annoying inner voice that likes to tell us that things won't work out the way we want them to. By getting these worries out and down on paper, it allows your inner voice to let go and it begins to get quieter.

15. Reduce your exposure to negative news stories. The media LOVES a bad news shocker, if it's really important your friends and family will talk about it. Get your "news" from blogs or special interest websites that you can subscribe to instead.

16. And last but certainly not least! Practice........ practice........ practice!

5 Coaching Tips to Eliminating Negative Thoughts

Do you consider yourself a pessimist? Or are you a pessimist but don't realize that you are? Well either way, thinking negatively affects you much more than you think. It affects all aspects of your life. We all have to deal with certain decisions and situations every day, and the best way to get through them is by eliminating negative thoughts. Everything in your life, from your attitude, relationships, work, and performance are affected by negative thoughts.

Avoiding negative thoughts is hard, even with the best intentions. Use these coaching tips to help you switch your way of thinking. These tips can help you see the world in a different and more positive way.

Tip #1 Concentrate on possibilities and not on impossibilities.

Most of the time, the cause of your pessimism is your focus on the seemingly "impossible" things that you need to do. When all you see are challenges, then it's no surprise that you're clouded with negative thoughts. Stay focused on possibilities! Don't think about how hard, impossible, or challenging your tasks are.

Tip #2 Eliminate negative words from your vocabulary.

Speaking negatively is going to bring you down. One of the first coaching steps you need to do is eliminate negative words from your vocabulary. Words like "can't", "impossible", "difficult", should be erased from your vocabulary. Think positively and speak positively to get rid of all signs of pessimism. No matter how tough things can be, there is always something positive to what you are going through. It is all about looking at the situation from a different perspective.

Tip #3 Be inspired

When it comes to coaching, inspiration is the key to happiness and success. Inspiration can be drawn by reading success stories of others who experienced the same thing you are going through. You can also read memoirs of successful people in your career. Seeing the challenges people faced and how they were able to overcome them will certainly inspire you. If they can do it, so can you.

Tip #4 Surround yourself with friends and family who think positively

Instead of being around people who think negatively, coaching will teach you to stick to those who think positively. Surround yourself with high-spirited, energetic, and inspiring people. You can learn from them, and you can share your experiences with them as well. This makes it a lot easier for you to get through whatever you are experiencing.

Tip #5 Do something for someone

Offering help to someone in need is one of the most liberating experiences. It will make you happy and make you feel good, too. You don't need to sulk in one corner and think negatively all the time. Do something good for someone by donating blood, visiting an orphanage, or even volunteering in a retirement home. There are so many ways for you to give back to the community and when you do, you will find that this is one of the best ways to inspire yourself.

These tips will help you overcome negative thoughts. When you're free of these guilty, uninspiring, and sad feelings, you'll be free to accomplish your goals and dreams in life.

The 4 Parter
Part One: Self-Belief

This is part one of a 4 part mini-course on how to build your self confidence. To make sure you receive each part as its published use the subscribe box on the left to have them sent directly to your inbox.

When it comes to creating a personal strategy for enhancing your self-confidence, it's important to concentrate on one particular area of your life at a time. There's no point tackling a number of different issues simultaneously, as you will only get bogged down with details. You'll end up with a very broad overview of the issues you face but without the insight that can be gained from taking one small step at a time. By focusing all your energies on just one area, you can really delve deep into the crux of the problem and take positive steps, before moving onto the next area of your life that requires attention.

A strong sense of self-belief is an essential quality to possess if you're looking to achieve a more self-confident personality. If you don't believe in yourself and your actions then it's difficult to expect others to believe in you. Self-belief can be infectious and you might be surprised at the effects that your own behavior can have on those around you. Self-belief can have such an impact on every area of your life that it's vital to try and enhance your attitude to yourself before you move on and tackle other issues relating to your confidence. From everyday actions like sticking up for your opinion in a discussion, to more long-term, life-changing decisions about career changes or relationships, you must employ a strong sense of self-belief in order to forward your goals.

Although your life is undoubtedly shaped by the world around you, you must learn to realize that you have the power to change your life in so many positive ways. By turning negative situations into positive life lessons and using bad experiences to help you grow stronger, you can build your confidence step-by-step. If you have issues of low self-esteem resulting from family conflict, understanding your sexuality, or dealing with negative attitudes from other people, then this is certainly the area you need to focus on.

Strong, decisive actions will demonstrate to yourself, and to others, that you have self-belief and that you are determined to carve out your own destiny. You must always believe that you are making the best decision for you and your life and never be afraid to argue your point. Your own actions and your own perception of yourself are the best tools for building your future. Self-belief can have such a strong influence on all areas of your life. Rather than hanging around in a job that's going nowhere and has no prospects, or staying with a partner through habit, your new sense of self-belief should give you the push to make serious changes to your life, in a confident and controlled way. After all, if you don't do something, no one else will.

Part Two: Body Language

To make sure you receive each part as its published use the subscribe box on the left to have them sent directly to your inbox.

Have you ever wondered why some people can enter a room and command a sense of power? They might not have spoken a word but their presence is sufficient to make everyone else sit up and pay attention. These individuals aren't necessarily tall, muscular or beautiful but they almost certainly have the knack of executing the art of positive body language.

Whether you're aware of it or not, you use body language on a daily basis to convey your feelings to other people. By learning to use your body language to your benefit, you can enhance your self-confidence and the confidence that others have in you. Body language can help you to achieve success in your career, your business dealings and in your personal life. By understanding body language, you can also gauge other people's perceptions of you and of the situations they find themselves in: in other words, you can read people.

Although body language is a science in itself and people have spent years studying and trying to unravel the exact nuances of non-verbal communication, there are definitely some key points to look out for when you're presenting yourself to other people. In obvious situations like conducting a meeting, confronting a partner, or going for a job interview, the need for affirmative and self-confident body language is imperative. However, as people get to know each other better then the more subtle aspects of their body language can help to reveal even more about their personalities.

Your eyes can say a lot about you and, in terms of coming across well to other people, direct eye contact is a safe bet. This is universally regarded as a sign that someone is being attentive and is interested in what the other person has to say. By looking someone straight in the eye you are giving the signal that you're being honest. Your arms are another giveaway when it comes to body language and this might be something you're not even conscious of when you're talking to others. By gaining some knowledge about the outward signs that your body uses to convey your emotions, you can then take positive steps to address these and try to portray yourself in a more confident and accessible manner. Crossed arms are a sign of defensiveness and this physical barrier that you are putting between your body and the person you are talking to can be detrimental in many situations. In contrast, holding your arms behind your back is a sign of confidence. So, next time you feel your arms itching to cross themselves, push them behind your back instead and watch your confidence levels soar.

The handshake is another body language sign that is open to much interpretation. As it's frequently used in situations that might have a bearing on your professional or personal life, make sure you get it right with a firm handshake that exudes confidence. Shake someone's hand with your palm facing upwards and you're submitting to their authority; palm down and you're trying to dominate. If you use both hands, then you might give the impression that you're a domineering character, so don't go over the top.

Part Three: Dress to Impress

This is part three of a 4 part mini-course on how to build your self confidence. To make sure you receive each part as its published use the subscribe box on the left to have them sent directly to your inbox.

Now that you've had a chance to think about self-belief and body language, it's time to take a look at your wardrobe. Although dress sense is very much a personal thing, the clothes you wear can say a lot about your personality. If you look good, you're more likely to feel good and you will naturally exude more confidence.

Dressing to impress doesn't necessarily mean breaking the bank with shopping sprees to expensive boutiques and designer shops. As the very appropriate proverb goes, "cut your coat according to your cloth". In other words, shop according to your budget. Having said that, some items of clothing are worth investing more money in and, depending on your line of work, you may wish to splash out a bit more for key pieces that will boost your confidence. For example, a tailored suit can be a fantastic investment. Whilst you might be lucky and find an off-the-peg suit that just happens to flatter your particular frame and figure, a tailor-made suit will give you that extra confidence boost when you really need it.

The art to dressing with confidence is to find styles and colors that really suit you. If pea green is your favorite color but you look like a bowl of soup when you wear it, then stop adding it to your wardrobe. Whilst no one wants to hide their personality away under bland clothing, there's a lot to be said for dressing for the occasion and a few classic items in your wardrobe will ensure that you have outfits at your fingertips whenever you need to look the part. An ill-fitting or inappropriate item of clothing will distract you and will also draw other's people's attention to areas of your body that might not be entirely confident with. If you spend a meeting or a first date tugging at a shirt that's just a little bit too tight around the midriff, your confidence levels will plummet and you won't be showing yourself off at your optimum.

If you're turning over a new leaf and ditching the contents of your wardrobe to start from scratch then take a friend with you when you go shopping. It's often a good idea to get a second opinion – just make sure it's an honest opinion. Whilst shop assistants can be very helpful, they're often busy and it's in their best interests for you to buy the clothes. A friend can also dash about to find different sizes and they'll probably pick out things that you'd never have considered trying if you were shopping alone. This can be a great way to broaden your clothing horizons and discover new styles.

If you can give yourself a confidence boost by dressing in clothes that suit your body shape and personality but are also comfortable and stylish, then you'll be off to a good start every day and this should have a positive impact on your work and other areas of your life.

Part Four: Learning from your Mistakes

To make sure you receive any future posts as they are published use the subscribe box on the left to have them sent directly to your inbox.

So, you feel good, you're acting the part of the confident individual and you look good, too. Now it's time to make sure that these feelings of positivity don't disintegrate the minute something goes wrong.

In order to really reap the benefits of increased confidence and self-worth, you have to accept that everything doesn't go according to plan all of the time. This has no bearing on you as an individual; it's just a simple fact of life. We all make mistakes: it's how we deal with them that counts. You need to try and turn a negative situation into a positive outcome and use the experience wisely in order to learn more about yourself and other people.

It can sometimes take a lot of courage to own up and admit to making a mistake, especially if it's one that has had financial or personal implications for other people, or the company you work for. By admitting to the mistake as soon as possible, you're demonstrating real confidence as an individual. The courage and humility required to do this will only serve to enhance your reputation in the eyes of others and it will also help you to gain closure on the event and move forward. Dwelling on the mistakes you make is a fruitless exercise and is simply time wasted that could have been put to better use.

Once you realize that you've made a mistake, the important thing is to try and rectify the situation as quickly as possible. Then, instead of thinking about how it could have been avoided if you'd done 'this' or 'that', think about how you can learn from the mistake and ensure that it doesn't happen again. If the mistake occurred because you were tired, or because you were becoming too blasé about a certain aspect of your job, then you need to look at these issues and decide on a plan of action to take away the reason for the mistake occurring.

The key is to evaluate certain aspects of your life in order to ensure that you don't keep on making the same mistakes. It's the person who fails to learn from their mistakes that will keep making them and, if you keep making the same mistakes, then your confidence will naturally decrease until you get to the stage whereby your peers and colleagues might begin to lose faith in your abilities. It can turn into a perpetual cycle and can have a detrimental effect on all areas of your life.

If, on the other hand you learn from the mistakes you make, you will discover areas of your life that you can improve. You have then succeeded in turning the negative situation surrounding the mistake into a positive outcome. This can only be a good thing when it comes to boosting your confidence and taking charge of your life and the path you're going to take.

FREE 30 DAY PERSONAL DEVELOPMENT COURSE

http://www.impactcm.co.uk/FreeCourse

Little Steps is an email course that gives you 30 actionable steps, one each and every day, to help you overcome the challenges you're experiencing in your life right now.

"Just wanted to say an enormous big thank you for this course. I have looked forward to the daily email, I've always appreciated them. I've learnt a fair bit about myself in the process and undoubtedly made progress in several areas." – **Simon**

"It makes life more manageable so that you don't feel overwhelmed" – **Julie**

"An exciting challenge each day" – **Michalis**

"I'm really starting to notice a difference my little steps are making. Mostly in the procrastination area but also to some extent in confidence as I've spoken to strangers more in the last 2 weeks than I ever would normally. Thanks for making the difference happen – little steps is so easy to follow" –
Lynne

http://www.impactcm.co.uk/FreeCourse

More Online
YouTube - Validation
YouTube – Validation.

http://www.youtube.com/watch?v=Cbk980jV7Ao

I'm just amazed at how great this video is. I laughed I cried, I'm so glad I watched it. Enjoy

Tell me about yourself, what is it you are interested in working on? What do you struggle with? What would you like to change or do better in the future?

Contact

Please feel free to contact me with any questions you might have, just email me directly

Email: paul@impactcm.co.uk

Telephone:

UK   0845 388 3218 or 020 7193 4411

USA   (928) 239-9149

Twitter: @impactcm

Facebook: http://www.Facebook.com/impactcm

CPSIA information can be obtained
at www.ICGtesting.com
Printed in the USA
LVOW10s1028190517
535143LV00020B/405/P